UNDECIDED

by Simon Fraser

Undecided

1st Edition: © 2015 Simon Fraser

This book was printed in the United States of America

Table of Contents

Dedication

For my parents,

Michelle and Robert Fraser,

For always pushing me forward when the world was
pushing me backward.

Preface

For most of my life, I had no idea what I wanted to do with my life. This was partly because there were so many things I was *supposed* to do.

Too many people hate their jobs. But they push through day to day, wasting their precious time on earth to pay for their kids' tuition.

That way, their kids, too, can go to college… get into debt… and end up working a job they hate so *they* can pay for *their* kids' tuition… and so on, and so on.

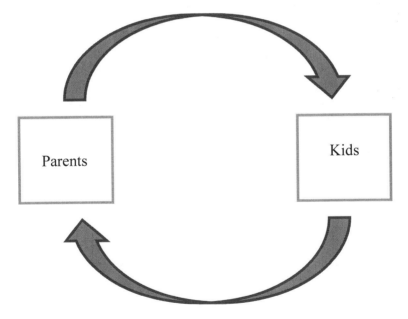

This is an arbitrary cycle that has gone on far too long. It locks creative, curious youthful people into a box of expectations, like jamming a spherical block through a

1

rectangular hole. To break this cycle, we must fully realize one simple truth:

College degrees aren't worth much anymore.

We must realize that experience, personality, and skillset are what defines a person – not exam scores.

We can break this cycle by empowering the younger generation to think for themselves and follow their passions.

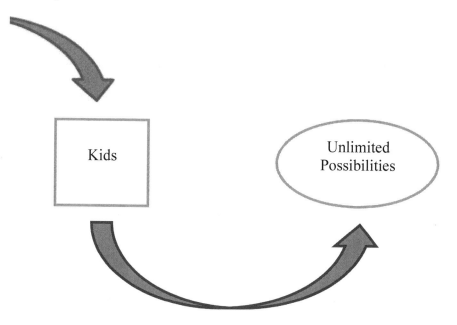

So my business partner, Ben, and I bought an RV to create this movement. We going straight to colleges around America, getting people to think and question the system they have mindlessly followed for decades.

To follow the movement, visit www.xplorflow.com.

~Simon

Introduction

I was standing outside of the library. It was mid-January and freezing. My hand and voice were both shaking, but not because of the weather. *I'm really going to do this*, I told myself. I dialed the phone, and listened to it ring.

………..

Instantly, an exhilarating wave of excitement, freedom, and opportunity rushed through my veins. *I did it. I dropped out of school*, I thought. *There's no turning back now.* I was only 19 years old, and I had no idea that this would turn out to be one of the best decisions of my life.

How can students be expected to plan their entire lives before the age of 20? Like many people, I have experienced this frustration firsthand.

As a generation, we are born and raised to plug ourselves into a specific system: go to college, get a job, work hard, and retire. Only after you "put in your time" can you retire and start doing the things that you love.

The system isn't perfect, and it definitely isn't meant for everybody. If you choose to go to college, you must get a job so that you can afford to pay back your student loans. If you hadn't taken out loans for a college degree in the first place, you wouldn't need a job to pay them at all!

Obviously you need a source of income to provide for yourself and your family. You also need a source of income to be a productive member of society. This book is here to tell you that going to college and getting a job is just one of many different ways to generate an enjoyable source of income for yourself.

5

If there are so many other ways, then why do so many students every year become shackled with student debt only to be forced to work a dead-end job for YEARS to pay back their loans after they graduate?

Some colleges have turned themselves into more of a profitable industry and less of an education system. As the price of tuition shoots through the roof, the value of a degree begins to fall. But somehow, millions of young people every year are flushed through this system of higher education with little or no direction.

When I was younger, I always hated the question: "What do you want to be when you grow up?" I never had a consistent answer, even a year into college.

Maybe you're in the same boat and feel anxious and overwhelmed, like I did. Maybe you're not sure what you want to do with your life yet, but you feel pressured to make a decision NOW. You see all your friends going to college, and it seems like everybody has their lives put together, except you.

The fact is, everybody feels that way. There are so many other options out there, and you don't have to be trapped into the system like everyone else.

This book will not only show you how to start finding your passions, but how to lead a successful life carving your own path. The truth is, there are no rules to life besides the laws of physics—only social expectations. After reading this book, you will know how to bend and break these expectations in order to find and follow your passions without submitting yourself to the same system that everybody else follows.

Undecided is filled with tons of secrets that colleges DO NOT want you to know about how their "business" is run. I will uncover how higher education has shifted its focus from educating young people to turning a profit, then share stories of people just like you who took the leap and now lead very successful lives doing what they love without a degree.

Again, this does not mean that college is a bad thing. It is only a bad thing if you do it for the wrong reasons. This book is about figuring out if, when, and why you should or shouldn't go to college.

When I was finishing high school, I felt exactly how you feel. I had absolutely no idea what I wanted to do with my life. So, I went to college without being ready or knowing WHY I was going.

I applied to five schools during my senior year of high school. During the application process, I remember scrolling through all the different options and thinking that most of them sounded boring or, even worse, useless. But, because of the way I had been raised, I still had no doubt in my mind that college was the only path to success. Choosing my major was the most difficult part of this process.

Seems backwards, doesn't it? I didn't realize it at the time, but I was going to college just to say that I did. This turned out to be a very expensive mistake.

I finally landed on Aerospace Engineering. My dad was an engineer, everybody knows it can be a high paying job, and I had always been pretty interested in flying planes. I was halfway decent at math, and it seemed like a challenge. So I thought, *What the hell, I might as well give it a shot. If I don't like it, I can always switch.*

After switching my major around a few times in college, I finally realized that I was on the wrong track altogether. I didn't care about my college classes because I wasn't learning what I wanted to learn. I was on a path that, for me, had no desirable end in sight. And the monthly student loan notices surely didn't help.

With the support of my family, I went against what everybody else was saying and dropped out of school.

Since then, I have dedicated my time to studying the flaws of the education system, and experimenting with lifestyle design and passion finding. With the help of an internship program, I was able to run over $300,000 in business before the age of 20, and mentor hundreds of college students to run their own businesses, allowing me to find my passion in entrepreneurship. In the past two years, I have learned and grown more than I ever did in college.

I have also interviewed several people who have succeeded by taking their own approach to life, and put the best REAL pieces of advice in this book. Everyone I have interviewed on the subject has experienced great success by using a variation of the principles that you are about to read.

These are not untested theories. They are not one man's guesses and opinions. They have been proven time and time again to help people find their passions and take their first steps toward success with or without a college degree.

After reading this book, I guarantee that you will have a much clearer idea of what you truly desire in life. You might decide that college is necessary for you (which is the case for some people), or you might decide that you want to be a chef, a writer, or a professional dancer. The possibilities are endless, and this book is the key that you need to not only find your passion, but to act on it.

Truly, anything is possible. By simply reading and following the steps in this book, you will be able to take your life wherever you want it to go.

My biggest regret?

That I didn't learn these concepts sooner. I would have saved over $60,000 in student debt, not to mention over a year of arbitrary studying. I would have found my passion much sooner, which would have saved me from wasting my time studying subjects I didn't want to learn in a way that I couldn't learn.

If you want to take hold of your future, learn from my mistakes and DO NOT WAIT. Each minute that passes is a minute you won't get back, so don't let it go to waste.

You already have two huge advantages on your side:

1) You are interested in success and strive to find and fulfill your desires.

2) The fact that you are reading this book already shows that you have the intelligence to search for tools to get you where you want to be.

Don't be the person who misses out on opportunity and happiness in life because they waited too long or worried too much about what other people would think. Be the person who people admire and emulate. Be the person who carves their own path. Be the person who takes action immediately and chases their dreams while everybody else stands by and waits for great things to happen to them.

What you are about to read has been proven time and time again to give people just like you a crystal clear vision of what they want their future to look like. After reading this book and identifying your desired path, you will know how to take action and put it in place.

In the first few chapters of this book, I will show how college is not right for everybody. I will discuss the little-known flaws of the system and explore how it has become more of a business than an education system. Then, I will lay out the steps that you need to follow to find your passion. Finally, I will give you the core principles you need to take that passion and use it to live the life you desire.

It's time to take hold of your own future. All you have to do to get what you want out of life is keep reading. Each chapter will leave you with a better vision of your own hopes and desires along with the principles required to take action NOW. Stop wasting time, take control, and enjoy creating the life you've always desired!

PART 1

COLLEGE

The System

We all grow up expecting to go to college. It's a system that we are programmed to believe works for everybody.

Study hard so you can get into college. Once you get there, study hard again so you can get a good job. Once you get that job, work hard so you can pay off your car, house, and student loans (all of which you wouldn't need if you didn't have a job in the first place). Eventually, the goal is to retire so you can start doing what you enjoy in your 60s.

> "What is the pot of gold that justifies
> spending the best years of your life hoping
> for happiness in the last?"   —Tim Ferriss

College enrollment in America has been rising consistently since the beginning of the 1900s. In 1940, 10% of people had been enrolled in college at some point or another. By 2009, this figure was 55%![1]

This is because employers are increasingly requiring bachelor's degrees for positions that never used to require them.

In 1940, you only needed a degree if you were going into a particularly technical field like engineering or medicine. However, 90% of people were still able to get jobs in management, administration, sales, etc. without a degree.

As of September 2014, 65% of secretary and assistant new job postings required a bachelor's degree.[2] The funny thing is that 19% of current jobholders in this field don't have a degree at all, but they seem to be doing just fine.

Has this particular job gotten more technically difficult? Not at all; otherwise, they would send the current assistants to get their degrees.

There is no specific major requirement; most job postings just say that you just need a degree of some kind. What is it about a college degree – any degree – that has just recently made them so valuable and necessary for people to do jobs that never required them before?

There is actually a word for this concept: *upcredentialing.* It would seem like degrees are getting more valuable because of their increased requirement; however, now that more and more people are getting them, the value of each one is decreasing. This is essentially inflation of college degrees.

Read this excerpt from a speech by Sir Ken Robinson, a renowned author, speaker, and international advisor on education in the arts:

> Suddenly, degrees aren't worth anything. Isn't that true? When I was a student, if you had a degree, you had a job. If you didn't have a job, it's because you didn't want one. And I didn't want one, frankly. But now kids with degrees are often heading home to carry on playing video games because you need an MA where the previous required a BA, and now you need a PhD for the other. It's a process of academic inflation. And it indicates the whole structure of education is shifting beneath our feet. We need to radically rethink our view of intelligence.[3]

There are several reasons for academic inflation, but it really boils down to one thing: as more people go to college, employers feel the need to keep up by raising job requirements.

The good news is, this is starting to change. People are finally realizing that college degrees are great ONLY for certain people aiming down specific career paths. For many others, struggling through college does nothing but waste time and money.

Realistically, 18-year-olds should not be expected to plan out their entire lives right after high school. Passions, likes, and dislikes all change constantly during the developmental period of 18-24-year-olds.

Maybe the concept of engineering, biology, or accounting seems exciting and interesting now, but that excitement could switch to something else at any time. People change their majors more than you think. Locking yourself into an expensive 4-plus-year commitment, while working toward one major, makes it very difficult to experience and test other potential passions.

On top of that, college is so expensive that if you do enroll, wasting even one semester in the wrong major can cost thousands of dollars.

Overall, this system is flawed in many ways and by no means right for everybody. Do your own due diligence and decide for yourself if the system of college fits with your passions and desires before committing to it.

---

[1] Robinson, J. A. (2011). The college bubble begins. The John William Pope Center for Higher Education Policy. Retrieved from

http://www.popecenter.org/commentaries/article.html?id=251
1

[2] Rampell, C, (2009. September 14). The college degree has become the new high school degree *The Washington Post.* Retrieved from http://www.washingtonpost.com/opinions/catherine-rampell-the-college-degree-has-become-the-new-high-school-degree/2014/09/08/e935b68c-378a-11e4-8601-97ba88884ffd_story.html

[3] Robinson, K. (2008). How schools kill creativity [Video transcript]. Retrieved from http://www.ted.com/talks/ken_robinson_says_schools_kill_cr eativity/transcript?language=en

Degrees

What is a Degree?

At its core, a degree is literally a piece of paper.

It provides written proof from your teachers saying that you learned everything in your major to their standards. This piece of paper will allow you to seamlessly plug yourself into the system. It will prove to employers that you can do your job competently, not to mention it makes for a great decorative piece in your office.

What does it take to earn this piece of paper?

If you haven't been through college, it goes something like this:

You sit through lectures for 4 years listening to different teachers explain their subject. You write papers on concepts, complete practice problems, and take quizzes and tests on your knowledge. These are all graded by your teachers or their assistants in order to determine how well you know the material.

Have you ever had a teacher who:

1. Didn't seem to care if you actually learned the material or not?

2. Was just flat out bad at conveying information in a relatable way?

3. Delegated most or all of the teaching to their assistants who weren't as qualified?

Teachers and professors are all different. In some cases, if you figure out their particular system of grading, you can easily ace the class even without learning much. In other cases, the teacher may be extremely passionate about what they do. Some of them make a huge impact on their students and become lifelong mentors.

But when you sign up for college classes, you're rolling the dice on which ones you get.

Correct me if I'm wrong, but at least some of your time in school has been spent figuring out ways to get a good grade, not actually internalizing and learn the material.

If I am wrong, then congratulations! You have successfully internalized all of the concepts, methods, and vocabulary terms. Not many people can do this, and college is probably a good option for you to maximize your potential.

But during school, have you actually put these methods and concepts into practice? Not an exam or test, I mean real-life practice? Because this is what you will be expected to do in the real world.

To learn—really learn—takes real-world experience. More on this in the next chapter.

Eventually, you will make it into the real world. If you go to college, you will have gotten your degree and will probably get a job somewhere. By this point, you've already paid tens of thousands of dollars and spent 4+ years preparing for this moment.

You will learn more *applicable* knowledge in your first month working a new job than you will in 4 years of college. This doesn't mean you won't learn anything in college—of course you will. However, most of the knowledge you learn in college doesn't directly apply to your career; thus, in a lot of cases, it is not realistically worth the amount of time and money that it costs.

Again, college is still right for some people. If your favorite subject in school was chemistry, it really makes you tick, and you get excited at the thought of researching chemistry, then college is probably going to be very valuable for you. If you've ever said your favorite subject in school was gym class, recess, or drama club, or if you didn't have a favorite subject at all, you're in a completely different boat. Figure out what you desire before you commit to college.

Have you ever seen the show "Are You Smarter Than a Fifth Grader?" If not, it is basically a game show where adults and fifth graders are asked fifth-grade-level trivia questions.

The adults always lose because they haven't used this information in years. Does this make them stupid? Not at all, they clearly lead fairly successful adult lives. I mean, come on, they're on TV! What this means is that apparently, they didn't need all of that information to be successful.

I'm not saying that children shouldn't go to elementary school. I'm just saying that, at some point in your life, you choose which channels of learning and practice you want to focus your energy on. A lot of the time, the general knowledge you learn about in different subjects in school ends up being useless when it comes to making a living doing something you enjoy.

The point is, before you spend all this time and money to earn this special piece of paper, find out what it is that you really desire first. Most 18-year-olds don't know what their true passion is, and haven't tried enough things to figure it out.

Either way, degrees are difficult and expensive to obtain. So if you're going to get one, make sure you're passionate about not only the process of earning it (i.e., reading and testing about your subject full-time for 4+ years) but also the job for which you need the degree.

Do you ever see older people in your college classes? There was always one or two in each of mine. They don't always fit in with the crowd because they're the ones who show up early, sit in the front, and leave late. They ask the most questions, and try to learn more than anybody else. They have figured out what they desire.

These people have already spent time in the real world experiencing different things. They eventually realized that what they need to fulfill their desire is a college degree. That's why they are making the most out of their resources in the college system. This is the much more efficient approach, as opposed to trying college first on a whim to see if it's right.

All in all, getting a degree equates to getting the approval of people who only know you through what grade you got in their class. Your actions, skills, and personality, things that are often hidden from your teachers, all define you far more than your grades do.

Learning

Learning—*true learning*—takes real-world, hands-on experience. You have to fail and make mistakes on your own in order to learn from those mistakes and actually grow. How did you learn to drive a car? To do laundry? Or even to speak English?

Yes, you do take a preliminary class on the rules of the road before you drive. But the first time you sit behind a wheel, even after learning everything in a classroom, you suck at it. The second time, you still suck. By the 5th time (hopefully) you've gotten a little bit better. You can't master the skill of driving by just taking the class.

You've never read a textbook on how to do laundry, you just tried it. You never took an English class as a child, you just listened and tried talking, failing miserably, until you got it right. If you practice enough doing something that is uncomfortable, eventually, it will become comfortable, just like throwing a football or a Frisbee.

If you ask any linguist, they will tell you the best way to learn any language is putting yourself into a situation where you have to learn it. For example, the best way to learn French is to go to France and try talking to people. You will start to pick up on the most important words at first, and get better with practice from there.

These are just a few examples, but this can be applied to everything in your life.

In the internship I did toward the end of my college career, I ran a $60,000 business over the summer. I had never run a business before, and I hadn't even taken any business classes. Regardless, with the help of a mentor, I grew and learned more than I ever could have imagined during the process.

I came out on the other side with a clear idea of how to run a business. I was much more confident and ready to take action than my friends who were taking business management classes at the time. The big difference? I had actually done it instead of learning about *how* to do it

Did I struggle and make more mistakes than they did?

Of course I did. But it was worth it.

I was constantly putting myself into new and difficult situations that made me uncomfortable or nervous. The more time I spent outside of my comfort zone, the more that zone expanded because what was uncomfortable at first became comfortable with experience.

I did things like going door-to-door, selling to customers, interviewing employees, managing people who were older than me, and much more.

The craziest part?

Through all of this learning, I actually made money. This didn't make sense at first because I had already spent a year *spending* money to learn.

I was given pointers and tips by my mentor before doing things like interviews for the first time, but I never took a class or a test on it. The real test was going out and trying it on my own. In my first interview, despite all the tips, I screwed up and stumbled over my words because I was so nervous. In the second interview, I did a little bit better. I kept trying and trying, and eventually, I got really good at interviewing just through consistent practice.

Interviewing is now one of my strengths. I never paid any money to learn how to do it; I just did it. Since then, I have completed hundreds of interviews for different candidates of various ages, all for different positions.

The first time I managed employees, I made the mistake of being the "nice guy." I let my employees take off early and show up late without repercussions because I wanted them to like me as a boss. This quickly caught up with me, and I realized work wasn't getting done, so something had to change.

I was forced to try things I never thought of trying before. I created consequences, positive incentives, replaced employees, and much more. It took about two months of trial and error before positive changes actually started to happen in my business.

Two years later, I'm in a position where I train other managers on how to lead and manage properly. And I still haven't ever taken a class on management!

If you try something enough, you can eventually turn it into a strength. Once you have several strengths, you can make money and create a living for yourself by using them in the right way. More on this later.

Notice a recurring theme here? This is how humans learn— by taking immediate action, which leads to trial and error. This process blooms into creativity, innovation, and growth. As Napoleon Hill said, "Strength and growth come only through continuous effort and struggle."

The main goal of the education system should be to learn—which, as we've established, happens best with mistakes and failures for most people. Instead, the ultimate goal in college is to pass your classes. In order to get good grades and pass the class, you must NOT make mistakes.

The learning environment that college creates requires reaching perfection without first struggling through the necessary process of growth to get to that point.

If the education system were structured to prepare you for real life, mistakes would be encouraged. Unfortunately, this is not the case, which is why so many kids in school are tempted to cheat to get a good grade and feign perfection. In a true, conducive learning environment, kids wouldn't feel the need to cheat. They would be encouraged to try, fail, learn, and repeat.

Everybody has their own method of learning that works for their personality. The structure of college is perfect for some people, but for others, it can hold them back.

When Gillian Lynne was in grade school, she couldn't concentrate because she always fidgeted. Her teachers were very worried and were convinced that she had a learning disorder. So, her mother took her to a learning specialist.

For 20 minutes, Gillian sat on her hands while her mother talked with this man about all of the problems she was having in school. This little 8-year-old had been disrupting people, constantly turning in her homework late, and creating other distractions.

Finally, the doctor told Gillian that he needed to talk to her mother privately. So, he turned on the radio that was sitting on his desk and left the room with her mother.

Standing outside, the doctor and Gillian's mother peered back in the window at the little girl. The minute they left the room, Gillian was on her feet, moving to the music. "Mrs. Lynne, Gillian isn't sick—she's a dancer," he told her. "Take her to a dance school."

On this experience, Gillian said: "I can't tell you how wonderful it was. We walked in this room and it was full of people like me. People who couldn't sit still. People who had to move to think."[4]

Gillian Lynne eventually auditioned for the Royal Ballet School and became a soloist. After a wonderful career, she founded her own company. She is now known for many famous Broadway productions such as "Cats" and "Phantom of the Opera."

This was all possible because she was put into an environment that encouraged creativity and learning in the way that that clicked with her. Someone with a different approach might have put her on Ritalin and told her to calm down.

Experience is always the best teacher, but everybody has their own way of learning. Surround yourself with people who are similar to you, like Gillian did. Take it upon yourself and read a book or an article that interests you. If you truly want to learn, your teacher shouldn't be the only one to tell you which chapters to read.

These days, you can learn just about anything you want just by looking on the Internet! Websites like YouTube, KahnAcademy, and Wolframalpha are available for free to teach students almost anything.

Use these resources to learn small bits of different things so you can determine which ones truly interest you.

For the right person, the specific learning process that college provides can be a perfect fit. For the wrong person, it can be detrimental.

---

[4] Robinson, K. (2008). How schools kill creativity [Video transcript]. Retrieved from http://www.ted.com/talks/ken_robinson_says_schools_kill_cr eativity/transcript?language=en

The Business of College

Tuition and Costs

Some colleges have turned themselves into a profitable business, putting their goal of education on the backburner. Tuition costs are through the roof, and colleges are making profits that are higher than ever. Milton Friedman, a Nobel Prize winning economist, estimated that most colleges could charge half of what Ivy-League institutions charge for tuition while still pulling a profit.

Average tuition costs are increasing at a rate much higher even than the inflation of the general U.S. economy. In 1977, the average tuition for private four-year colleges was less than 17% of the average family income. In 2012, this figure had risen to over 32% of the average family income.[5]

In a typical industry marketplace, this amount of inflation would not last long. It would quickly be eliminated and regulated by competition. However, organized collusion between colleges regarding how much tuition they will charge has allowed colleges to continue to strip students and families of the consumer protection they deserve.

Colleges are able to control their own competition, continue to charge more for tuition, and create a collective monopoly over the industry of students.

Why is the cost of tuition rising so much, and how have more people been able to afford it even with these outrageous cost increases?

When asked about the tuition increases, Carl Rogers said, "The cost of any institution is largely determined by the amount of revenue it can raise." Now, Professor Rogers is no critic of the education system. He has been revered as "the supreme defender of higher education."

Breaking this down, we find that the total amount of money an institution pulls in from government subsidies, endowments, donations, etc., determines of how much they charge for tuition, and how much they can spend that year—NOT the other way around. In other words, they receive most of their funds before determining their budgets.

Most businesses first determine their costs (expenses), then determine what profit they want to make, THEN set their prices. This way, the business can avoid over-inflating the value of their products, so they can pull in an accurate amount of revenue needed to cover for all of the expenses and the desired profit.

Colleges pull in money from several different mediums. Tuition is a big one. On top of that, they consistently ask for donations from alumni, collect revenue from sports, publicity, endorsements, taxes, and more.

Using sports, commercials, school pride, and overall publicity, colleges consistently represent themselves as institutions with education as their #1 priority. This is not always the case.

So what do colleges do with all of this extra money that they don't always need? They probably spend it on hiring and training the best teachers, refining curriculums, and state of the art laboratories for research, all to help the kids learn and prepare for the future, right? I mean, that is their top priority...

Not quite.

Most of the time, they either plunge it back into their biggest money-makers like sports, or spend it on less-than-necessary things that will increase their revenue for the next year. Here are some "costs" that may be driving your tuition prices up:

Ohio State University bought over 1,100 iPads to give to the student athletes in 2013.

The president of the University of South Carolina spends $879 per night for hotel rooms while traveling, and, in one year, spent $7,000 on chauffeur services.

Former Stanford President Donald Kennedy used $2,000 of this money each month to pay for the flower arrangements in his home. These flowers were meant to accent his $3,000 cedar-lined chest (also paid for by tuition). When Mr. Kennedy got remarried in 1987, tuition dollars also paid for part of his $17,500 wedding reception.[6]

Now, these are isolated examples, and not all colleges are this extreme. The point of bringing up these examples is to show the flexibility of the word "cost" when used to justify tuition increases. Colleges too often add expensive activities like this, and call them "increased costs" later.

When asked about these costs, the Dean of Bowden College said, "People would come forward with plans that were good ideas—and because it was a period in which we could afford to grow, we just said yes without being very deliberate about it."

Students and their parents continue to struggle, sometimes drawing equity on their home just to afford tuition costs and lock into unforgiving student loans. What these consumers don't realize is that this extra money doesn't always cover the increased cost of educating their children. It is often used to fund of the unnecessary and expensive fantasies of faculty and administrators.

This corrupt business model continues to thrive partly because it is thinly veiled by the altruistic cause of supporting and educating our youth.

Student Loans

One of the main reasons tuition costs are allowed to continuously rise is the extreme availability of student loans. These easily-accessible financial aid programs give students a way to feel like they can still afford college despite the rising tuition costs.

Total student debt in the U.S. has gone from $241 Billion to $1.1 Trillion from 2003 to 2014.[7] This is an INSANE increase in such a short period of time.

Student loans are incredibly easy to apply for. You can have little or no credit history and still get approved for financial aid. The typical financial rules of risk do not apply to student loans. In college, I was denied a $15,000 car loan even after I had already been approved for a $60,000 student loan.

These loans are handed out like candy because the creditors know that the loan must be paid back no matter what. They never go away. Even if a student dies, the remaining balance will be transferred to the closest relative instead of being forgiven like most other debts.

One time, I tried to set up an automatic monthly payment for one of my federal loans. While I was on the phone, the representative went on to explain that even after the full balance is paid, they would continue to charge me the monthly payments unless I manually cancelled the automatic payment manually.

In another instance, my brother successfully set up an automatic payment over the phone for a separate private loan. A month later, he received a late fee and a threatening notice in the mail. After promptly paying the late fee and trying again to set up an automatic payment for a second time, he was charged another late fee the month later.

For whatever reason, the system didn't confirm the automatic payment request, but didn't bother to notify him.

Not every college and financial aid provider operates exactly like this, but it is eye-opening to see how easily things like this can happen when it comes to student loans.

Agencies liberally hand out financial aid, but show no mercy when it comes to collecting their dividends, even sometimes at the expense of the students and their families. The inflated value of a degree and empty moral priorities of colleges perpetuate this corrupt system and allow colleges to continuously exploit the "gold mine" of college students year after year.

---

[5] Median incomes v. average college tuition rates, 1971-2012. (2014). Retrieved from http://college-education.procon.org/view.resource.php?resourceID=005532

[6] Sowell, T. (1993). *Inside American education.* New York, NY: Free Press..

[7] Davis, G. T. (2014, September 23) Student loan debt and the threat to American homeownership. *Huffington Post.* Retrieved from http://www.huffingtonpost.com/garrick-t-davis/student-loan-debt-and-the_b_5865774.html

Decide

By now, you have learned a lot about how the business of college is operated and perpetuated. While it is important to point out these processes, keep in mind that college is not all bad. There are so many different ways to learn and prepare yourself for the future, and college is just one of them. For the wrong person, it can feel like shackles holding them back—but for the right person, it can be the best way to unlock true potential.

No matter who you are or what situation you are in, YOU have to decide for yourself which path you want to take.

Yep. Nobody else has the answer, and you can't find it on Sparknotes.

Getting a degree is a HUGE investment of time and money; two resources that are often limited. So, before you decide what to spend them on, you must first know what you desire.

I'm talking big picture. Not what you want for your birthday, not what you want for lunch tomorrow, but what do you actually want out of life?

Action Tip #1

Ask yourself that question right now. What do you want out of life? I'm serious. Sit down and write a couple sentences that come to mind when you ask yourself this question.

If you don't have an answer for this question yet, don't worry; you aren't expected to. Just being conscious of the question itself is a step in the right direction.

Everybody desires different things, which is why this is such a difficult question to answer. At this scope, if you ask enough people, you will notice some common themes. Freedom, happiness, love, and making an impact are some that are often sought after.

Personally, I'm a big freedom seeker. I want to have as much freedom as possible—to be able to do whatever I want whenever I want.

Some people want to give and feel as much love and happiness as possible with the people around them.

But this isn't about them, or me—it's about YOU.

If you start at the highest level and ask yourself what you ultimately desire in life, narrowing the scope becomes easier. Eventually, you can narrow it down enough to figure out what you should do each day to achieve your ultimate goal.

Again, you don't need a single answer for this question. Desires change, and chances are you want a lot of different things out of life. The next section will help you narrow that focus to find out what you are truly passionate about.

For now, I want to focus on a good friend of mine, Ben Arwine. Throughout his experience, he has successfully found one of his passions and created a life that allows him to practice it every day. I've learned a tremendous amount from his story and I know you will too.

Before Ben went to college, he had no idea what he wanted to do with his life. You might be able to relate to that.

Currently, he is finishing his degree in Entrepreneurship, and he has successfully run $300,000+ in profitable businesses. He is currently the president of a prestigious business fraternity, has mentored hundreds of college students, and has also worked with nonprofits and startups around the world.

When I asked Ben what college had done for him, he told me the biggest benefits for him were the opportunities outside the classroom. These opportunities allowed him to try several of his interests firsthand in order to test his likes, dislikes, strengths, and weaknesses. The goal of playing the field like this was to give him a better idea of his answer to that big question—what does he ultimately want out of life?

From his experiences and opportunities, he found one of his passions to be leadership. Specifically, he likes the feeling of making a positive impact on the people around him.

I asked Ben how he knew that leadership was his passion. He went on to explain that first, he was able to throw himself into the fire and take on different leadership roles. After trying it several times, he said it was a gut feeling more than anything. A gut feeling of being excited about what he was currently doing in the moment.

Ben wouldn't have found the opportunities that led him to his passion if he hadn't tried college. While he agrees that it isn't for everybody, he also recognizes that it can help people find their passions too like it did for him.

During our conversation, we discussed how he attempts to answer the big question, and he gave a version of the following advice:

Think about when you're at your best. What are you physically doing at that moment? What about when you're the most happy? It is necessary to ask yourself these questions, and you must have the self-awareness to realize when you're doing something that brings out the best in you or that you enjoy so much that hours fly by like minutes. When you realize it, keep doing it.

Ben realized that he was happiest when he was making a positive impact on the people around him. He was only able to come to this realization because he created the opportunity to try it, and had the self-awareness to analyze his emotions.

Action Tip #2

So ask yourself right now—what are you doing when you're at your best? When are you happiest? Delve into every last detail of your answer.

You might be surprised what you find out about yourself by simply asking the right questions and taking the time to ponder them.

Throughout this process, remember that this is not a science. There is no exact formula that will spit out a correct answer for what you should do with your life. Things change constantly, so ALWAYS keep an open mind.

Regardless of where you are right now and what your overarching goals and desires are, I am going to show you how to find the best possible next step to get you closer to answering the big question for yourself.

Every idea in the next part of this book has been tested by either myself or other people who have successfully created a life tailored to their ultimate desires. Learn from them as I have; apply these ideas to your own life, and enjoy finding your passion.

PART 2

PASSION

What do you want to be when you grow up?

There are millions of different paths to take in life, and now you know that college may not be right for you. You also know that you don't have to go to college if you don't know WHY you plan on going, despite all the pressure around you.

So, what now? With so many paths to take, how do you choose the right one? This section will show you how to find your own path and how to take the first steps down it. This is where the fun stuff starts.

There are SO many options out there besides college, it's not even funny. Who knows where you'll end up? One thing's for certain: It's NEVER too late to find your passion. The fact that you're reading this book is evidence enough that you're on track to find it sooner rather than later.

Some people are lucky enough to know their calling at a very young age. But you probably aren't in that same boat. You've got to work harder to find it, but that's okay because you'll be much better off for it.

When I was a kid, I was the same way. Grownups always asked me, "What do you want to be when you grow up?" I hated this question more than anything. I had no idea, and my half-hearted answer changed every time somebody asked.

The truth is, that's the wrong question to ask in the first place. You shouldn't be asking yourself what you want to be. Stop focusing on the end result and start focusing on the journey that takes you there.

Remember how experience is the best teacher? This is so important because what you do in your life is not just a means to an end. The process itself is what makes you better and helps you figure out where and how to find your fulfillment.

Instead of asking yourself what you want to be, ask yourself, "What would I not mind struggling through to achieve?"

The value is in the journey, not the destination. Once we reach our destination, the euphoria of accomplishment is short-lived. Almost immediately, we feel the need to set our next goal and start striving for it. Realize that true fulfillment comes from growing and learning throughout the journey, not from arriving at your destination.

You must enjoy the journey. That's where you spend your time. If you don't enjoy the NOW, or what you're doing day-to-day, you're not only limiting your growth but you're also striving toward a goal that's not worth reaching.

For example, maybe you have always thought about being a famous musician. It seems like it would be great, and it probably would be. But first, you must realize what it actually takes to become a famous musician. In this case, it entails years and years of practice and long hours every day, playing your instrument.

So, ask yourself before you take the first step toward this goal:

"Would I not mind years and years of practice and long hours every day, playing my instrument to become a famous musician?"

If you get excited by this thought and truly love the process of practicing music in that capacity, then go for it with all your might. You will have an amazing and fulfilling journey.

If, however, you determine that the idea of being a famous musician isn't worth the necessary time and effort, then focus on your other dreams first because you aren't as passionate about this one.

I'm not saying that you should give up on your dreams just because they are difficult to attain. In fact, that's the opposite of my point.

Shifting your focus from the end result to the process is just a fool-proof test to help you determine which dreams you are truly passionate about. The sooner you do that, the sooner you can start focusing on the ones that mean the most to you.

A girl named Mai Lieu once went to college to become an accountant. After trying it out, she realized she couldn't imagine a life surrounded by numbers. So, she dropped out and became a beautician, something she loved to do and was very good at. She eventually quit her job to become an inventor of beauty products, and is now a successful millionaire, author, and inspirational speaker.

Maybe you want to be a writer. You love putting thoughts down and creating stories in your spare time after grinding through each day at your 9-5 office job, but being a full-time writer doesn't seem *practical*. There is risk involved:

45

you may get writer's block, people might not like your stories, nobody will publish your work, and the sun might as well be in your eyes too.

If you feel this way and would gladly struggle through writing each day in your spare time to become a writer, stop making excuses and go for it as soon as possible!

Action Tip #3

To get organized, write down each of your goals, or things you'd like to be or achieve. Then, write down the process that it will take to reach each of them.

For each item, ask yourself "Would I enjoy struggling through the process so that I can achieve this?" Write "yes" or "no" by each one, then cross off all the ones that you said no to. After you've narrowed it down, you should know which goals you think will fulfill you the most.

Remember that things always change. Just because you crossed off certain items doesn't mean you are ruling them out forever. At the same time, just because you have one main goal now doesn't mean it will end up being your true passion. Be sure to repeat this exercise every few months to keep you on track.

The thought of doing something is always different than actually doing it. So start practicing your instruments. After taking action, if you realize that you aren't being as fulfilled as you thought you would be, do not get discouraged. Stop, and move on to something else.

You have one short life to live. When you die, everything you've ever learned and everything you've ever owned all disappear. The only things that remain are the impacts you made on the world and people around you with your *actions*. So why would you spend even a single second doing something that doesn't make you or somebody you love happy? This is your true legacy.

Don't use your already wasted time as an excuse to waste more time. You can break free, and you can create any life you want. We all have our own goals and aspirations. Find out what yours are and act on them immediately. Continue to question your desires, continue to evaluate your actions, and never stop searching.

> "Everybody should... in their lifetime, sometime... consider death. To observe skulls and skeletons and to wonder what it will be like to go to sleep and never wake up— never. That is a most gloomy thing for contemplation. It's like manure. Just as manure fertilizes the plants and so on, so the contemplation of death and the acceptance of death is very highly generative of creating life. You'll get wonderful things out of that."
>
> —Alan Watts

Desire

"Desire is the starting point of all achievement, not a hope, not a wish, but a keen pulsating desire which transcends everything."

— Napoleon Hill

Everything begins with desire. Any invention, idea, lifestyle, business, career, or friendship always starts as a simple desire. Even this book was merely a desire of mine a few months ago!

I'm not talking about a wish or a want; I'm talking about a true, burning desire. Once you know exactly what this desire is, you will be subconsciously prompted to act on it. That's the easy part.

Edwin C. Barnes was an ordinary man who had always dreamt of becoming the business partner of Thomas Edison. He was one who could accurately describe his desire to work with Edison as an obsession that consumed his thoughts.

After many years of obsessing over the thought of working with Edison, he finally made his way across the country to the famous inventor's office. He pleaded to help with something—anything!

Starting with a broom in his hand, he waited 2 years for his golden opportunity. He eventually rose up in the company and became Edison's partner in sales, and achieved his dream!

There were so many employees in the company who wanted to work closely with Thomas Edison. Many of them had worked there for 10+ years, and were in positions much higher than a janitor. Why was Barnes able to move from his low position to being Edison's partner in only 2 years?

The only thing that separated Barnes from any of the other employees who wanted to work closely with Edison was the strength of his crystal clear burning desire to do so. He wanted it more than anybody else in the factory; thus, he naturally put more time and energy toward that desire than anybody else in the factory.

Everybody has this level of desire inside of them somewhere. Finding it is the tricky part.

The most important questions to ask when trying to define your desire are:

1. What excites you? It could be anything. Don't limit yourself to things that typically make money like jobs or careers. Think of your hobbies, sports, animals, interactions with people, etc. What is it that you look forward to each day? What do you think about or long to do while you're busy doing things you don't enjoy?

2. What would you do if money were no object? If you didn't have to trade 8 hours a day to pay your bills, what would you spend your time doing?

3. What occupation would you do for free just for the joy of doing it?

Action Tip #4

These are difficult questions to answer. Keeping them in mind, try this exercise:

Set a timer for 10 minutes to do a free-write. Writing freely opens up doors and connections in your brain that you never knew existed. Focus on the questions above, and start with writing down the first answer that pops into your head. If you can't think of anything, write about that. The key is to keep writing nonstop for 10 minutes straight. You will be surprised at what you find out about yourself. I have done this countless times, and believe it or not, the desire for me to write this book started with a free-write.

Remember, your goal is to find an enjoyable process that you can spend your time doing. Keep in mind that you will learn from these experiences over time and eventually be able to use them to your advantage.

ANYTHING counts, as long as it is something that excites you. Continue questioning your actions, and once you are aware of that excitement, keep taking action.

Do it as often as you can. Use your spare time. Surround yourself with people who have the same desire. Join online and face-to-face groups and communities to plug yourself into the culture of people who share that particular desire.

It doesn't have to feel like your #1 passion right away—in fact, it probably won't feel like that. Just do something. Just as trial and error is incredibly important when learning skills, it is also NECESSARY when learning what your passions are. You will either develop a stronger passion for it or realize that it was never your passion.

Either way, you've made great progress. You have either found your passion or ruled out something that you thought might be it. The only mistake you can make is to not do anything.

Keep the story of Edwin C. Barnes in mind. He was able to act toward his desire so easily and efficiently because of the true strength of his desire. Taking action on your desire will become second nature only after it becomes a "keen, pulsating desire which transcends everything."

Finally, it is important to remember that there is not an exact science to finding true desire. For some people, it can take a day, but for others, it can take years. The key is to try everything, take action quickly, and never stop searching.

Review on Desire:

1. Desire is where everything starts. It is necessary to have a clearly defined burning desire if you want to take the steps toward living your fulfilling life.

2. Finding your desire can be difficult, but it is doable. Use tricks like free writing, and asking yourself the right questions in order to unlock a genuine emotional response, then use your emotions to find out which activities really excite you.

3. Start somewhere. Don't wait for the perfect fit, because the only way to find it is to act now and embrace failures—the same way you learn any other skill.

4. Never stop searching.

Using Passion

There is not much more to finding your passion. It's not a science, and, ultimately, it is up to YOU to put these tips into action and decide.

While it can be very difficult finding your passion from scratch, the first step to progress is defining and asking the right questions.

The reason you are reading this book is to find the answer to one question:

What is your passion?

Breaking this question down, you are able to open up new perspectives and angles of thinking.

So what are you doing when you are at your best? Passion can be defined in many ways, but it always includes a mix of personal strengths and enjoyment. Think about what activities you're physically doing when you are at your best in terms of both personal strength and enjoyment.

It is necessary to have the self-awareness to realize when you are at your best so you can tailor your actions accordingly.

You can look at the big question from so many different angles.

What would you not mind struggling through to achieve?

This puts the focus on the journey, not the destination. Instead of just aspiring to be something, you are able to recognize that you gain fulfillment by spending time becoming something. Only then can you easily choose what to do each day to gain success and happiness.

Finally, do not forget that every great thing starts as a desire. It must be a keen, pulsating desire in order to prompt meaningful action. The first step in acting on your passion and unlocking its true potential is to continuously fuel it and allow it to occupy your mind.

Now I want to focus on a different friend of mine, also named Ben.

Ben Cummings grew up in Michigan and ran a small landscaping business in high school with some friends. He, like many others, went to college because he thought he was supposed to.

He spent most of his time in college skipping class to work on his landscaping business. One day, he was in the library, brainstorming names for his business, and that's when he finally realized that he was on the wrong path.

He became self-aware and realized that he was at his best when he was being creative with his business. After that moment, he resolved to drop out of school and grow his business full time, because he knew it was one of his passions.

Now, his company is pushing $500,000 in revenue, and he makes a decent living for himself, while being able to pay several full-time employees as well. He spends time on the side working on other small entrepreneurial endeavors and is always enjoying life.

Ben told me he was never worried about not having immediate income because he knew that his burning desire to make his business succeed and his intense work-ethic would carry him as far as he wanted to go.

I asked Ben what advice he would give to people who were struggling to find their passion and get on a path that would lead to happiness and freedom. Paraphrasing, here is some of his advice:

Finding something you enjoy is the first step. After you know that, try to see if you can make money doing it. Whether it's selling a service or spreading knowledge, there is always a way to make money with a skill.

You have to try as many things as possible. Your passion won't come easily, and it won't come at all if you don't actively seek it out. You will know when you are closing in on a passion. It will be a gut feeling that tells you to keep doing it. Never stop looking, and remember that failure, not success, is what creates progress.

And finally, always be better than yesterday.

What can we learn from Ben's story?

He decisively acted on a desire once he knew it meant a lot to him. He still had doubts but acted anyway because he knew it would prompt growth. It was difficult at times, but he always kept pushing forward.

No, you don't have to drop out of school and start a landscaping business to be happy and successful, unless you're like Ben.

But you do have to follow your passion. Too many people go through the motions of life without ever experiencing all that it has to offer. Like Ben said, the first step is finding out what you enjoy—what excites you, what makes you tick.

Do not do the most realistic and practical thing you can think of. Listen to your heart, not your head.

> "Realistic is the most common path to mediocrity."
> —Will Smith

We have learned in this part of the book that a keen, pulsating desire will prompt action subconsciously, but if your passion is not at this level yet, don't worry. The principles and techniques in the next section will help you build on your passion and develop it into the burning desire that will prompt easy action. You will have to work harder at the beginning, but I guarantee that you will be better for it in the long run.

Now that you know how to start finding and defining what you are passionate about, the next step is using it to unlock your true potential. The principles in the next section will show you how to break free and use your new passion to take action and create the life you desire.

PART 3

FREEDOM

Apathy

A mentor of mine once told me about an interesting concept called the 20-40-60 rule. It goes like this:

20-year-olds care too much about what people think of them. Once they hit 40 years, they realize that they never should have cared in the first place. But only after 60 years do they TRULY not care about other peoples' opinions of them!

The biggest roadblock between you and your dreams is the fact that you care too much about what people think of you. This is the #1 reason people don't go after their dreams in the first place, and have regrets once they finally reach that 60-year-old mentality.

If you practice the maturity and mindset of that 60-year-old enough, it will eventually become habit. Only then will you will be able to take action on your desires without much internal resistance.

As a society, we create social standards that act as "rules," based on the fear of others' opinions of us. Everybody has a vivid picture inside their heads of how they want to be seen by others. Often, this image is of a person who is talented, wise, and outgoing. The problem is that most people don't end up making that mental image into a reality.

Why?

Fear. We are afraid of stepping outside these artificial social norms that we've created for ourselves. In a sense, we are trapped by our own beliefs. This is a scary concept, but if viewed in the right way, it can be very freeing.

The truth is, all rules outside of science and law can be broken without compromising ethical and moral standards.

The bad news is that we are caged by our own beliefs. The good news is that we are the only ones who ultimately control these beliefs. With the right mindset, you can consciously break these barriers down and turn any mental image into a reality.

Tim Ferriss, entrepreneur, world traveler, and author of *The 4-Hour Work Week,* introduced me to the concept of comfort challenges. These are exercises meant to force you outside of those comfortable social norms. Just like a muscle, the more you are stretched outside of your comfort zone, the bigger that comfort zone grows. Here are a couple of comfort challenges in Tim Ferriss's book:

Comfort Challenge 1: Get Phone Numbers

For two days straight, get three phone numbers from random people of the opposite sex that you find attractive (girls, this means you too). How many times do you walk down the street and see somebody attractive and want to talk to them? What is stopping you from doing it? Probably a voice inside your head saying something like: What if he/she thinks I'm a weirdo? All that means is this is the perfect opportunity to take that step past your fear of worrying about what other people think. Yes, there is a chance he or she will think you're weird, in which case that doesn't matter because you probably won't ever see that person again. Plus, it makes for a funny story to tell your friends! However, I've found that most people are pleasantly surprised and flattered by your confidence. Here's how Tim Ferris does it:

"Excuse me, I know this is going to sound strange, but if I don't ask you now, I'll be kicking myself for the rest of the day. I'm running to meet a friend, but I think you're really cute. Could I have your phone number? I'm not a psycho—I promise. You can give me a fake one if you're not interested."

Comfort Challenge 2: Relax in Public

This one can be quite fun. Two days in a row, go to a random crowded place. Coffee shops, libraries, and sidewalks all work. Simply lay down on the ground and relax for 10-30 seconds. Make sure to get comfortable and pretend like nobody is watching. This is best to do with a group of friends. If somebody asks what you're doing, just say you felt like relaxing for a second. The more weird looks you get, the better. Thinking outside of the box is great, but if you really want to take your life by the reins, you need to get used to acting outside of the box.

Yes, these sound cheesy, but trying to step out of your comfort zone is SO important. It will give you a feeling of being uncomfortable at first, but once you break through that feeling, it immediately turns into relief and confidence.

When you finally start shooting for the stars, people WILL doubt you and try to hold you back. It's the only way they know to keep you from out-hustling them and leaving them behind.

Too many people live their lives abiding by guidelines that are shaped by people who are unimportant in their lives. You have one short life, so live it for YOU and nobody else.

The only reason I didn't drop out of school sooner than I did was because I was afraid of what people would think of me. I *knew* that my friends, people who didn't know me, and old high school acquaintances would view me as a dumb kid who was going nowhere in life.

As soon as I realized that I was foolish to let those opinions affect my life, I decisively acted on my desire. I dropped out of college, and I haven't looked back since. I could have saved myself so much extra time, money, and stress by reaching that level of maturity sooner.

Not to my surprise, a lot of people acted just as I was afraid they would. They looked at me weird, told me I would fail, and doubted me to no end. However, along with the pall of gloom cast by those knuckleheads came a wave of support from people who really mattered to me.

Parents, relatives, and close friends—people who *really* matter—desire only one thing for you: your happiness. If you can convince them that pursuing your passion, whatever it is, will make you happy, they will support you 100%. Keep this in mind when determining who to spend your energy on, and who you should forget about.

When you see a picture of yourself and a group of friends on Facebook, the first thing you do is analyze how you look. If it's an embarrassing picture, you probably feel uncomfortable, knowing everybody is seeing it. In reality, everybody else in the picture is just looking at and analyzing themselves too. Why spend your energy worrying about what these other people think when they're only worrying about themselves?

Most people don't care about you. The sooner you realize and accept this fact, the sooner you can free yourself from the chains locked by insignificant opinions.

This is another truth that seems devastating, but when you look at it in the right way, it is incredibly liberating. Imagine not ever having to care about what people think about you! The possibilities are ENDLESS.

> "You wouldn't worry so much about what others think of you if you realized how seldom they do."
>
> —Eleanor Roosevelt

Getting a college degree is a perfect example of this everlasting quest for approval. You put your degree on your resume so that future interviewers can determine your worth based on your professors' assessment of your grades.

Why can't you show them yourself? Somewhere inside of you is a unique set of skills and abilities that nobody else has. Maybe you've found them; maybe you haven't yet. Force yourself to get up, find out what they are, and do something with them. You do not need the approval of anybody else to chase your dreams.

Fear and Action

"Inaction breeds doubt and fear. Action breeds confidence and courage. If you want to conquer fear, do not sit home and think about it. Go out and get busy."
—Dale Carnegie

Fear is the paralyzing emotion that separates you from people like Steve Jobs and Richard Branson. These people that we idolize as role models were once young kids with the same doubts and fears that we all have. Only after they let go of their fear and decided to take action did they begin achieving massive success.

Carving your own path is scary. You naturally ask yourself questions like:

What if I'm not smart enough? What will people think if I fail? What if I'm just not capable?

These questions go through everybody's mind when they start challenging themselves and dreaming of a better future.

Perhaps the most powerful feeling above is the fear of failure or rejection. You've had this feeling before—your stomach churns, you start sweating, and you feel your heart beating faster and faster, pumping adrenaline through your veins by the second.

This nervous feeling is almost identical to the feeling of pure excitement. If you play or watch sports, you know exactly what I'm talking about.

These feelings are so similar, and your mind is so powerful, that you actually have the power to consciously turn nervousness into excitement. Olympic and professional athletes have mastered this.

It's an incredible feeling.

All it takes is immediate action. Once you push through that initial fear without thinking about it, the negative feeling of nervousness turns into a positive feeling of relief and excitement. This creates confidence, fuels your drive, and forces you to grow.

Besides, what is the absolute worst thing that can happen if you try something risky?

Failure.

We already know that every failure is simply an opportunity to learn and prepare yourself to succeed the next time around. Realize that the worst that can happen really isn't that bad, then take immediate action. Planning and forward thinking are great, but they are both worthless without action and follow-through.

> "Success is not built on success. It's built on failure. It's built on frustration. Sometimes it's built on catastrophe."
> —Sumner Redstone

Find what you desire, rid yourself of fear, and force yourself to act on it. Your success won't come immediately, but action ALWAYS leads to progress—in the form of many failures and many successes.

The timing will never be perfect. There will always be a better scenario in your life when you have more money, more time, or more motivation—but if you sit around and wait for that perfect scenario, I promise it will never come. Successful people achieve their dreams by creating that time, money, and motivation with action, not by waiting for them to magically appear in front of them.

Once you take action, you start a snowball that will create opportunity—in the form of time, money, and motivation.

There are a million excuses for why you shouldn't do something.

Feel like you don't have the time? Do a detailed time management analysis of how you spend every minute of your day to find out where you're wasting time. Thousands of people have made their dreams come true in their spare time. Aspiring authors write while they're eating or riding the bus or train. Set aside an hour per day to focus 100% of your efforts on your passion.

Feel like you don't have the money? Try crowdfunding. Thousands of people have pitched their ideas and have received billions of dollars (a projected 34.4 billion in 2015) from investors because they had a passion, a burning desire to accomplish something, and they communicated that passion to others well enough that investors wanted to be a part of their dream.

People are defined by their actions, not their thoughts. You can be the most motivated and driven person in the world, always talking about how you're going to do this or that, but none of that matters if all that talk doesn't lead to actions.

> "So, what will your mark be? The time to decide is now. Find what you are passionate about and strive to be the best at it. Do not

let it cross your mind that you do not have what it takes to pursue your dreams."

—Kendall Wernet

Mindset

A mentor of mine once told me that your money lags 12 months behind your mindset. Once you fixate your mind to focus toward your goals, you will naturally start achieving them. This goes back to turning a want or a wish into a keen, burning desire.

This principle is IMPERATIVE to beginning on your path to massive personal success. Once you get into the right mindset, all you have to do is keep your focus and start crossing off the days until your new life is financed.

What does it mean to have the right mindset?

Mindset means two things:

1. You have a crystal clear vision of where you will be in the future.

2. You KNOW deep down that this vision is a reality, but it just hasn't happened yet.

This vision generates clear subconscious goals in your mind, which allows you to focus very easily on them. In a way, you are conditioning yourself to constantly feel the need to make your vision a reality.

When I did my internship in college, I had a goal of running a $60,000 business. Everyone who hit that number got to go on an all-expense-paid awards cruise at the end of the year.

Immediately, I fixated my mind on earning the cruise. So I set off and got right to work. I set my computer desktop and cellphone screen backgrounds to a picture of a cruise ship to keep reminding me of my goal. Each time I looked at my phone or computer, that big boat would stare into my soul, taunting me and forcing my imagination to run wild.

I would often zone out and imagine what the cruise would be like, picturing different specific scenarios that could happen. When I would talk with the other interns, we would laugh and joke and wonder together about what the vacation would be like. After about a month of working toward my goal and consistently envisioning the cruise that I had come to desire so much, the picture of the cruise I had been obsessing over had morphed into a very vivid, colorful, and clear vision in my mind.

By that point, I knew I had to be there. It had become real, and it was no longer a dream or a distant desire. I HAD to find a way to make it on that ship. From that point on to the end of the summer, I had no doubt in my mind that at some point in the near future, I would be staring off into the dark blue waters of the vast ocean, basking in the warm sun, and sharing iced drinks and stories with my fellow interns.

Needless to say, that September, I spent three days on that cruise ship having the time of my life.

Once you apply this mindset to your vision, it truly becomes a reality. At that point, the only thing between you and your goals is time.

There are several key takeaways that we can learn from this story:

First, I started working toward my goals immediately. This not only gave me confidence and progress, but it helped my vision further develop in my mind because I was doing activities that I knew were pushing me closer to my goal.

Second, I surrounded myself with people who had similar goals. The other interns had all desired the same thing, and, as I spent more time with them, our visions collectively became much clearer.

Third, I didn't reach the point of absolute certainty right away. It took about a month for my mindset and vision to mature and sink in. The key is to be patient but very persistent when picturing and working toward your goals.

To put yourself in the perfect mindset, your vision has to be something that you know with absolute certainty. Until that point, it is merely a dream that seems out of reach.

Every vision starts as a desire. Keep your desire in mind and take the time to turn it into a vivid movie in your head.

Think about something you know with absolute certainty. For most students, graduation is an easy example. If you are in high school or college, you probably have a clear vision of graduation in your mind. Close your eyes and take 30 seconds to picture your upcoming graduation. Pretty easy, right?

It's easy for a several reasons:

First, you are already taking classes and working toward that goal of graduation. Each day, you push yourself closer and closer.

Second, you are constantly surrounded by people with the same vision and goal of graduation, in classes, with your roommates, with your friends, etc.

Third, you realize that graduation is in the future, but you remain patient and persistent. This vision that you have didn't magically appear when you were born. It became clear only after you started taking your classes and working toward it with the people around you.

Sound familiar?

The exciting part is that you can apply these same principles to any goal in your life. This will begin the process of molding your wants or wishes into a keen, pulsating desire that will subconsciously prompt meaningful action.

As long as you apply all of the above three principles to your goal, I guarantee your mindset will be in the right place within a month. Once your mindset is at that level, start crossing days off the calendar because 12 months later, your life of ultimate freedom and happiness will have begun.

Right now, set a timer for 20 minutes. Sit down and imagine where you want to be in the future. With the tips from Part 2, you should by now have a good idea of some of your desires.

Don't just think about them, imagine several vivid and detailed scenarios about situations you might find yourself in. Keep this colorful vision in your mind and expand on it for 20 minutes until it feels real. This can be very fun.

Repeat this every day. It doesn't have to be for 20 minutes every time, but hold yourself accountable by finding something that will remind you of it at least once each day. For me it was setting my backgrounds to pictures of a cruise ship.

Now, start working toward your vision. If you can't work on it full-time, do just one thing today that will push you closer to your goal. Then do the same thing tomorrow and the day after. To get your mindset to the right place, it is necessary that you start working toward your goal immediately.

Next, surround yourself with people who have similar goals. Find people who want the same things out of life and talk to them as much as possible. This will speed up the process of getting your mindset to the right point.

Finally, be persistent. Work toward your goals and replay your vision in your mind every day. All it takes is one activity each day.

Mastermind

"You are the average of the five people you spend the most of your time with."

—Jim Rohn

To achieve your desires, it is NECESSARY that you spend your time with people who will push you forward, not hold you back.

Once you have your desire in mind and you are developing your vision, seek out people who have similar desire and goals. Talk with them and hang out with them as much as possible. By spending more and more time with people who are like how you envision yourself to be, you are opening up your true potential.

This group of five people fuels your passion more than you possibly can by yourself. Imagine talking to a friend about something that excites you, but the friend has no interest in what you are saying. They will respond with short, unstimulating phrases, and, before long, you will feel like you're speaking to a brick wall. At this point, it almost seems like they are sucking the excitement out of you. This is the opposite of progress!

Now, imagine you are talking to a friend who shares the same level of excitement about the subject. They respond with new ideas, smiles, and laughter, pouring fuel into your passion, which will prompt action and progress.

By discussing your goals and making them public to like-minded people, you are giving yourself an extra layer of accountability. As crazy as it sounds, you will accomplish your goals to avoid embarrassment. Nobody wants to tell their friends that they didn't do what they said they would do. Also, if one or more of your friends have the same goal, there can be an element of competition involved. Competition will push you forward.

These people will present new ideas that you might never have come up with. The expression "two heads are better than one," could not be more true (as long as the two heads are on the same page). Imagine what five heads can do!

Andrew Carnegie built a multi-billion dollar steel industry in the late 19th century. It is a little-known fact that Carnegie himself did not know the first thing about steel. So how was he able to build one of the most successful businesses in history without knowing much about his product?

He realized the importance of surrounding himself with the right people. He understood that he didn't know how to make steel, and resolved to find people who did. He found people who knew what he didn't know and who had the same astronomical goals that he did.

Carnegie's mind alone could not create the steel empire that he dreamt of, but he knew that if he put himself next to the right people, that "mastermind" group would turn his dream into reality. He pushed these people toward their goals while they pushed him toward his.

Imagine you want to learn to play the cello. You've always been into music, but you live in a house full of computer science engineers with completely different passions. Every time you play your cello, your roommates ask you to keep it down, eventually making you feel guilty for wanting to practice your cello.

Now, imagine you live in a house full of other aspiring musicians who each has his or her own instrument to learn. In this scenario, every time you practice your cello, your roommates will encourage you. Every time you don't practice, they will challenge you, pushing you forward.

Needless to say, this creates a much more enjoyable and productive environment.

If you want to turn your passion into a living, or if you want to fuel it even more, it is necessary that you ditch the friends who are holding you back. If they aren't pushing you forward, they are holding you back.

It's very difficult to cut ties with close friends, but the overwhelming feeling of freedom and the tremendous progress that it will bring is well worth it in the long run.

Now, write down names of the five people you spend most of your time interacting with. Ask the following question for each of them:

Does this person act how you would like to be?

For the ones you said yes to, find a way to spend more time with them. The more time you spend with them, the more you will be like them.

For the ones you said no to, ditch them. Think of another person who acts how you would like to be, and resolve to talk to them at least three times a week.

You will see positive changes in your life very quickly.

Persistence

The world is full of needy people. If you fill the needs of the people around you, you will make money. Plain and simple.

Just as finding your passion starts with desire, making money with your passion starts with desire. As long as it is a burning desire and you are consistently working toward it, money will follow.

Every passion can be turned into a source of income. There are three primary things that can be provided to society in order to make money:

1. Knowledge

2. Service

3. Product

Your passion will fall under one of these three.

Let's say you have a passion for flying planes and desire to one day become a commercial jet pilot. Usually, it takes many years of training before pilots are able to fly commercial jets.

So, pilots who aren't yet at this point will use their knowledge to make money in order to continue doing what they love. Most of them will become flight instructors, filling the need of other aspiring pilots. Obviously, this was only possible because they took action and started working toward their passion, getting better at it with each failure.

Or maybe you love rock climbing, but it doesn't seem practical to get a job at a climbing park. It probably wouldn't pay much either.

First, if getting a job at a rock climbing park doesn't sound compelling, it might be more of an enjoyable hobby than a burning passion. In this case, keep trying new things.

Second, don't limit yourself to getting a job. There are so many ways to make money with your passion. You could advertise your own climbing lessons for people, charge them to go on guided trips with you, or sell climbing gear.

You can create a business out of any passion in the form of knowledge, a service, or a product. You do not have to be an expert in your field, and you do not need a PhD to teach people what you know. People benefit from other peoples' stories, knowledge, and skills—you just have to be better and more knowledgeable than the general public and fulfill a need in order to provide value.

There was a man in the early-mid 1900s who never liked working for anybody. He started a successful restaurant in a small Kentucky town for several years where people loved his fried chicken recipe.

A new highway was built that carried traffic out of the way of the restaurant, so it eventually went out of business.

The man retired shortly after. Soon, he realized that after pouring endless passion into his chicken recipe for his entire life, all he had to show for his hard work was a $100 social security check each month.

He grabbed a piece of paper and a pencil, found his shotgun, and made his way to his back porch. He began writing his suicide note, while listening to the peaceful stream behind his house in the background.

While writing, he came to the realization that he was only in his 60s, and he had many years ahead of him. He had a choice to either die right there or keep working toward his passion.

So he did the latter. He drove across the country for two years, pitching his idea to restaurant owners, sleeping in his car most nights. After getting 1,008 nos in a row, the 1,009th restaurant finally said yes.

It was that decision on his back porch that allowed the man to finally achieve his dreams. There are now over 18,000 KFC restaurants around the world, all using Colonel Sanders's secret chicken recipe he felt so passionate about.

Put it in your mind that you will stop at nothing to create the life you deserve. Work each day toward your passion, and NEVER quit.

Call to Action

About 15 months before I wrote this book, I was in the worst situation of my life. I had somehow dug myself into a hole of $60,000 of tuition in a year and a half, and found a way to gain almost no value from what I was supposed to have learned during that time.

I had no direction, and, even worse, I had done nothing about it.

That January, my brother, Eric, called me up and told me he was dropping out of school. I knew he had been feeling the same way that he was about both of our situations, so I wasn't too surprised.

But up until that moment, I had no idea that dropping out of school was even an option. When I heard that from him, my mind bent in all sorts of directions. After I finally settled down and got over the frustration that he had thought of it first, I immediately knew what I was going to do the next day.

I knew I wanted to run some sort of business, but I didn't feel like I had any "golden ticket" ideas. Though I was afraid to admit it to myself at the time, I didn't think I was capable of actually starting a real business either.

I had a job mentoring students to run the same business I had run the summer before, but I was running low on cash, so I decided to get a job at a restaurant to pay the bills. The job sucked and I quit after a couple months. The only reason I didn't quit sooner was because the food was great, and I got a free meal each shift.

In the meantime, I immersed myself in stories about successful entrepreneurs, reading every book I could get my hands on about the subject. I wanted to be like Richard Branson, but I still didn't have the confidence. So I kept dreaming and I kept reading.

Week after week, and month after month, the desire to start my own business gradually grew inside of me. My vision of being a serial entrepreneur got clearer each time I imagined it, which continued to fuel my desire even more.

It took about a year of letting this vision and desire boil and churn inside me before it exploded. I was so frustrated that I hadn't done anything about it. What was once a distant dream had eventually morphed into a keen, pulsating desire that subconsciously prompted action. Using some advice from friends and mentors, I decided to write a book.

Since then, my brother and I have also started marketing a new business, with several other ideas in the works. I still have a long way to go, but I finally took the first step on my path. All it took was desire, vision, and time. It would have been much easier if I forced myself to take action sooner, but what I've learned is that any desire and vision will prompt action, given enough time.

In the past couple of years, I have truly learned the importance of allowing desire to consume you. If you want to live passionately, that is the first step.

I know there are people like me out there, and that's why I wrote this book.

DO NOT underestimate yourself like I did. You can decide to do whatever you want in life. You can give any excuse, but I promise the only thing standing between you and your dreams is you.

Thank you for reading *Undecided,* and allowing me to share my story with you. You are the reason I get to continue chasing my passion, and I hope I was able to help you chase yours.

Book Recommendations

The Four Hour Workweek by Timothy Ferriss

This is one of my favorite books of all time. A lot of the ideas in my book are taken from The Four Hour Workweek. Ferriss does a great job explaining how you can ditch the 9-5 schedule, earn ultimate freedom, generate passive income, and use it to do whatever you want in life.

How to Win Friends and Influence People by Dale Carnegie

This book is the best resource you can possibly use to improve relationships with the people in your life.

The Alchemist by Paulo Coelho

The Alchemist is a fictional story about a boy who sets off on a quest to find a treasure that keeps appearing in his dreams. It is the best allegory out there for passion-finding.

Think and Grow Rich by Napoleon Hill

Napoleon Hill spells out the best fool-proof method of forcing yourself to accomplish your dreams. All the potential is in your own head, and this book will be the one to help you find it.

URGENT PLEA!!

Thank you for buying my book!

I appreciate all of your feedback, and I love hearing what you have to say.

I need your input to keep improving.

Please leave a helpful REVIEW. You can access the book at www.businessofcollege.com.

Feel free to reach out to me personally with any comments, questions, or to share any success stories! You can reach me at scfraser4@gmail.com.

Be sure to check out www.xplorflow.com for the latest events and products we are releasing.

Thanks!!

~ Simon

Acknowledgements

Samantha Sabihi: Thanks for choosing an awesome book title even though I doubted you at first.

Ben Cummings & Ben Arwine: Thanks for taking the time to share your stories and allowing me to share them with everyone else.

Christian Chasmer, Chandler Bolt, and Hunter Freeman: Thanks for the mentorship, advice, and support while I was writing this book.

Eric Fraser: Thanks for always holding me accountable and always building me up.

Mom & Dad: Thanks for the endless support and advice.

Olivia & Abby Fraser: Thanks for always being so sweet.

The Student Painters Family: Thanks for the support and the incredible experience you gave me. This never could have happened if I hadn't gotten through the summer of Stu Paint.